To Kai,
May you see what
I see!

John Bender 2007

May 2007   With Love from Grandma & Grampy Peters ♡

Do You See What I See?

By Claudia Cangilla McAdam
Through the Camera of John Fielder

kids
WESTCLIFFE PUBLISHERS

westcliffepublishers.com

International Standard Book Numbers
ISBN-10: 1-56579-554-7
ISBN-13: 978-1-56579-554-9

Editor: Jenna Samelson Browning
Cover Illustration and Book Design: Anna-Maria Crum
Production Manager: Craig Keyzer

Published by:
Westcliffe Publishers, Inc.
P.O. Box 1261
Englewood, CO 80150

Printed in China by Hing Yip Printing Co., Ltd.

Library of Congress Cataloging-in-Publication Data:
McAdam, Claudia Cangilla.
  Do you see what I see? / by Claudia Cangilla McAdam ; through the camera of John Fielder.
    p. cm.
  ISBN-13: 978-1-56579-554-9
  ISBN-10: 1-56579-554-7
  1. Nature photography--Juvenile literature. I. Fielder, John. II. Title.
  TR721.M28 2006
  508.022'2--dc22
                            2006018023

For more information about other fine books and calendars from Westcliffe Publishers, please contact your
local bookstore, call us at 1-800-523-3692, or visit us on the Web at **westcliffepublishers.com**.

I dedicate this, my first book for children, to my son J.T. (1980-2006). Though his ashes have returned to Nature sooner than most, his lifetime was filled with the joy of discovering Nature's mysteries. He appreciated the microcosms of the miracle of life on Earth perhaps more than things conspicuous and grand.

John Fielder

In memory of my father, Lou Cangilla, who taught me to see the shapes in the clouds.

Claudia Cangilla McAdam

Straws filled up with milky sips?

Paper shredded into strips?

Q-tips stacked like kindling sticks?

Icing smeared on birthday cake?

Ripples on a frothy lake?

Blanket spread for coldest days?

Snowfield wrapped in purple haze.

Candy sucker, sticky sweet?

Juicy slab of uncooked meat?

Fabric draped in graceful folds?

Red rocks solid, grand, and bold.

Wisp of smoke afloat on air?

Grandma's silky, silver hair?

Lint picked from a pair of socks?

Water rushing over rocks.

Alligator's bumpy hide?

Mold on food long set aside?

Rugged, rubber running track?

Granite pushing life through cracks.

Elephant's rough, wrinkled back?

Chunk of lava, charcoal black?

Storm clouds quickly growing dark?

Trunks of weathered, peeling bark.

Cotton candy wound up tight?

Bridal veil so airy white?

Ghostly image—scared to peek?

Misty cascade in a creek.

Marble shot with skill and grace?

Earth as seen from outer space?

Coral dotting deep blue seas?

Canopy of aspen trees.

Golden sheen of lion's coat?

Rusting side of fishing boat?

Wildfire flames that windstorm whips?

Autumn's kiss on aspen tips.

Chugging choo-choo's engine light?

Earring set with diamond bright?

Monster's scary, staring eye?

Moonset in a starless sky.

Rainbow sherbet, creamy cold?

Easter eggshell, brightly bold?

T-shirt worn in tie-dyed craze?

Mountain sunset sky ablaze.

Claudia Cangilla McAdam

During the past three decades, Colorado author Claudia Cangilla McAdam's work for adults and children has appeared in scores of magazines and newspapers throughout the country. She has won awards from *Highlights for Children* for both her fiction and nonfiction, and she has authored or co-authored eight previous books, including *Portraits of Character* and *The Christmas Tree Cried*. A nature photography enthusiast herself, she was drawn to Fielder's photos and inspired to pen the text of this book. She invites you to visit her website, TwoSonsPress.com.

John Fielder

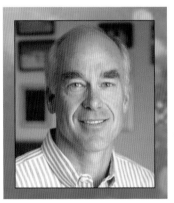

Colorado-based John Fielder has been photographing the natural world since 1972. He has worked tirelessly to promote the protection of his state's open space and wildlands. His photography has influenced people and legislation, earning him recognition including the Sierra Club's Ansel Adams Award, the University of Denver's Daniel L. Ritchie Award, and the Distinguished Service Award from the University of Colorado. He speaks to thousands of people each year to rally support for timely land-use and environmental issues. He is the photographer of 37 exhibit-format books and guidebooks. To learn more, visit johnfielder.com.